FLORIDA'S BUBBLING SPRINGS

JOAN LUNDQUIST SCALPONE

Published by

MINI DAYTRIP BOOKS

PHOTOGRAPHY
by
Joan Lundquist Scalpone

CONTENTS
Springs of Florida

		Page
1.	ALAPAHA RISE	7
2.	ALEXANDER	7
3.	BECKTON	8
4.	BLUE Gilchrist County	8
5.	BLUE Jackson County	9
6.	BLUE Madison County	9
7.	BLUE Volusia County	11
8.	BLUE Lafayette County	12
9.	BLUE HOLE	12
10.	BOZELL	13
11.	BRANFORD	13
12.	CHARLES	14
13.	CHASSAHOWITZKA	14
14.	CONVICT	15
15.	CRYSTAL	15
16.	CRYSTAL RIVER	16
17.	CYPRESS	17
18.	DE LEON	18
19.	ELLAVILLE	19
20.	FALMOUTH	19
21.	FANNIN	20
22.	FERN HAMMOCK	20
23.	FLETCHER	21
24.	GAINER	22
25.	GINNIE	22
26.	GREEN COVE	23
27.	GUARANTO	24
28.	HAMPTON	25
29.	HART	25
30.	HOLTON	26
31.	HOMOSASSA	27
32.	HORNSBY	27
33.	HUNTER	29
34.	ICHETUCKNEE	29
35.	JUNIPER	30
36.	KINGSLEY LAKE SPRING	30
37.	KINI	32
38.	RIVER SINK	32
39.	LIME	32

40. LITHIA 33
41. LITTLE RIVER 34
42. LITTLE SALT 34
43. MANATEE 35
44. McBRIDE SLOUGH 36
45. MORRISON 36
46. NAKED 38
47. NATURAL BRIDGE 38
48. NEWPORT 39
49. OTTER 40
50. PEACOCK 40
51. POE 41
52. PONCE DE LEON 42
53. RAINBOW 43
54. ROCK 44
55. ROYAL 44
56. RUM ISLAND 45
57. RUNNING 45
58. SAINT MARK'S 46
59. SALT 47
60. SILVER 48
61. SILVER GLEN 48
62. SUWANNEE 49
63. TELFORD 50
64. TROY 50
65. VORTEX 52
66. WACISSA 52
67. WAKULLA 53
68. WALDO 54
69. WARM MINERAL 55
70. WEEKI WACHEE 56
71. WEKIVA Levy County 56
72. WEKIWA Orange County 57
73. WHITE 57
74. WORTHINGTON 58

TUBING TRIPS 59
MAPS 59-63
BEST CANOE RIVERS (For Spring Hopping) 64

3

INTRODUCTION
SPRING FACTS

Florida has 300 known springs with 27 being FIRST MAGNITUDE. These discharge together over *6 billion gallons daily.* Florida leads the world in 1st magnitude springs and quantity of FLOW.

It took me *2 years to research this book.* It was never boring. "Spring Hoppers" enjoy inexpensive entertainment as a great number of the boils are *free* and open to the public. Others are state or county parks with nominal entrance fees. I have visited 175 springs and found each to have a beauty of its own!

About 70 springs are SECOND MAGNITUDE and 190 classed as THIRD MAGNITUDE or less. Springs such as Rainbow, Wakulla and Silver are the source of large RIVERS. Suwannee River Valley has 50 springs, 9 of which are First Magnitude.

★ ★ ★ ★ ★ ★ ★ ★ ★ ★ ★ ★ ★

CLASSIFICATION BY MAGNITUDE
M G D = Million Gallons Daily

MAGNITUDE	AVERAGE FLOW
1	64.46 M G D or more
2	6.46 M G D
3	.64 M G D
4	100 gallons per minute
5	10 gallons per minute
6	1 gallon per minute
7	1 pint per minute
8	Less than 1 pint per minute

★ ★ ★ ★ ★ ★ ★ ★ ★ ★ ★ ★ ★

The Florida Aquifer is made of thick LIMESTONES and conducts enormous quantities of water throughout our state. It is often *cavernous* containing (wet and dry) caves of immense size such as the system networking the Chipola River called FLORIDA CAVERNS. This is the most *wondrous natural GEM* in the state of Florida!!

A total of 16 SUBMARINE SPRINGS are located offshore (mostly in the gulf). Their openings issue from limestone and discharge from below *sea level.* Some are seen at tide stages by the visible "boil". The FLOW of some of these submarine springs is great enough to reduce the "salinity" of surrounding seawater!

TARPON SPRINGS in Pinellas County is the best known submarine spring. It is 160 ft. long by 60 wide...deepest point is 125 ft. Tarpon Springs was connected to huge LAKE TARPON by way of a SINK and underground channel. The extreme depth (115 ft.) of these channels was most unusual! Late summer of 1950 Tarpon Springs had a flow of 646,000,000 million gallons daily. In May of 1969 a dam was built around TARPON SINK which prevents ordinary draining and refilling of the lake. Today the spring no longer flows.

★ ★ ★ ★ ★ ★ ★ ★ ★ ★ ★ ★ ★

NUMBER OF FIRST MAGNITUDE SPRINGS BY STATE

State	Number	Rock
FLORIDA	27	Limestone
IDAHO	14	Limestone, Basalt
OREGON	15	Basalt
MISSOURI	8	Limestone
CALIFORNIA	4	Basalt
HAWAII	3	
MONTANA	3	Sandstone
TEXAS	2	Limestone

In Charlotte County on Burnt Store Road 7 miles south of Punta Gorda are the HOTTEST springs in Florida appropriately named HOT SPRINGS. The artesian well flowed at 97° F. The drilled well was 1,578 ft. and discharged about 3,000,000 gallons daily to a swim resort in 1965. Spring is now capped and on private property... Springs and acreage are for sale for $5,000,000 (more or less) ..... Any takers??

During my "spring hopping" I found that 10 springs were named BLUE SPRINGS. This became *confusing* unless you designate the county where all these BLUE'S are located! ALAPAHA RISE and HOLTON SPRINGS were the *most remote to locate* as they were in deep forest near Suwannee River. SPRING CREEK SPRINGS in Wakulla County is the most unique due to the fact it produces the largest flow of (both) FRESH and SALINE water in the state.

So many spring NAMES will remain a mystery as to their origin but they all lend intrigue to the lovely boils.... I especially enjoyed RUM ISLAND, MYRTLE'S FISSURE, NAKED, COFFIN (shaped just like one), IDIOT'S DELIGHT and PEACOCK SPRINGS!!!

SPRING FACTS

U.S.A. has 78 first magnitude springs. FLORIDA has 26 of them (the most) of any state.

Florida's 1st Magnitude Springs	County
1 ALAPAHA RISE	Hamilton
2 ALEXANDER	Lake
3 BLUE	Jackson
4 BLUE	Madison
5 BLUE	Volusia
6 CHASSAHOWITZKA	Citrus
7 CRYSTAL RIVER	Citrus
8 FALMOUTH	Suwannee
9 FANNIN	Levy
10 GAINER	Bay
11 HOLTON	Hamilton
12 HOMOSASSA	Citrus
13 HORNSBY	Alachua
14 ICHETUCKNEE	Columbia
15 KINI	Wakulla
16 MANATEE	Levy
17 NATURAL BRIDGE	Leon
18 RAINBOW	Marion
19 RIVER SINK	Wakulla
20 SAINT MARK'S	Leon
21 SILVER	Marion
22 SILVER GLEN	Marion
23 SPRING CREEK	Wakulla
24 TROY	Lafayette
25 WACISSA	Wakulla
26 WEEKI WACHEE	Hernando

ALAPAHA RISE

1ST MAGNITUDE   FLOW 409 MILLION GALLONS DAILY

DESCRIPTION 73°

Even though it is one of Florida's "biggest bubblers" most people have never heard of this GRANDDADDY SPRING!

Deep (40 ft.) vent rushes up to a LARGE COFFEE COLORED POOL. *Hills* and oak woods cover the land surface.

SPECIAL FEATURES AND USE

Stream run is only 300 ft. and pours into the SUWANNEE RIVER. Because of the *pristine location* it is seldom used.

LOCATION   Hamilton County
Access from Suwannee River, 21 miles northwest of Live Oak, FL, Rd. 249

ALEXANDER SPRINGS

1ST MAGNITUDE   FLOW 78 MILLION GALLONS DAILY

DESCRIPTION 76°

The 200 ft. wide pool is a favorite with SWIMMERS and DIVERS ALIKE because of its *roomy pool* and sandy beach. Water depth over cave is 25 ft. and the lengthy "spring run" (15 MILES) flows into the ST. JOHNS RIVER.

SPECIAL FEATURES AND USE

U.S. Forest Service operates a varied recreational complex here. There is CANOEING, CAMPING, SWIMMING, DIVING, SNORKELING and hike trails…. I thought the area most SCENIC!!

LOCATION   Lake County   Open To Public
6 miles southwest of Astor, FL off Hwy. 19
In OCALA NATIONAL FOREST   *(904) 669-3522*

BECKTON SPRINGS

2ND MAGNITUDE   *FLOW 25 MILLION GALLONS DAILY*

DESCRIPTION 70°

Dense foliage provides side canopies to the *perfect circle pool* of 175 ft. by 100 ft. "Ten foot" high banks mix with low Cypress areas. The "run" is only 3 ft. deep drifting a short distance to HOLMES CREEK.

SPECIAL FEATURES AND USE

Boil spews from *cracks* between GIANT BOULDERS. Beckton is a relaxing spot used by local residents for "cooling down" and fishing. CANOE TRIPS.

LOCATION   Washington County   Open to Public
From Hwy. 79 north of Vernon 2 mi, Vernon, FL

BLUE SPRINGS

2ND MAGNITUDE   *FLOW 45.5 MILLION GALLONS DAILY*

DESCRIPTION 72°

Occupies a depression in dense forest and swamp 900 ft. from SANTE FE RIVER. A *giant stone ledge* drops 25 ft. to a small cave orifice. CLEAN CLEAR WATER affords fine underwater photos. TAME FISH greet swimmers. A combination of submerged BOLD CLIFFS and aquatic plants create *underwater magic!!*

SPECIAL FEATURES AND USE

You may stroll a 1500 ft. boardwalk or enjoy CAMPING. Nearby, 450 ft. to the east is NAKED SPRING...yes, there's a story here...!! Blue Springs is a commercial resort and most scenic!!

LOCATION   Gilchrist County   Open to Public
9 miles west of High Springs, FL Off SR 340

BLUE SPRING

1ST MAGNITUDE   *FLOW 186 MILLION GALLONS DAILY*

DESCRIPTION 70°

Main spring flows into MERRITTS MILL POND. Many other springs and "sinks" feed the pond on its 4 MILE ROUTE. Divers have reported the area "honeycombed" by CAVES and TUNNELS *hundreds of feet long* and near 300 ft. DEEP!! Springs empty into CHIPOLA RIVER.

SPECIAL FEATURES AND USE

Used irregularly throughout the years as a resort. CITY OPERATES swimming facilities. Water discharge from MILL POND is used for *electric power*. While in the area DO TAKE THE OPPORTUNITY (just 3 miles away) to visit FLORIDA CAVERNS. Its intriguing NETWORK of CAVES will leave you in awe!! It is a 1783 acre *LOCAL PARK*. Open May to October.

LOCATION   Jackson County   Open to Public
Marianna, FL On Hwy. 164
Florida Caverns   *(904) 482-9598*

BLUE SPRING

1ST MAGNITUDE   *FLOW 94 MILLION GALLONS DAILY*

DESCRIPTION 70°

Youngsters were cavorting in the chilly 30 ft. aquamarine boil the day I visited. Very *steep stone banks* border the 25 ft. deep pool which passes on to the WITHLACOOCHEE RIVER.

SPECIAL FEATURES AND USE

It is still in a *pristine state*. Lots of natural ROCK and many paths lead to the boil. RAINBOW COLORS ripple out putting on "a show" for visitors. A kind of *peninsula* around the water gives great views. Finding the Spring was easy.... Leaving was difficult....BLUE SPRING is a shining medal in Florida's treasure chest!!

LOCATION   Madison County   Open to Public
10 miles east of Madison, FL on Hwy. 6 Southwest corner of Withlacoochee River Bridge.

BLUE SPRING (JACKSON COUNTY)

BLUE SPRING (MADISON COUNTY)

BLUE SPRINGS

1ST MAGNITUDE   *FLOW 104.8 MILLION GALLONS DAILY*

DESCRIPTION 74°

Circular pool is 100 ft. wide with steep banks. Depth is 42 ft. and water shimmers GREENISH-BLUE tones. "Run" is one half mile flowing into the mighty ST. JOHN'S RIVER.

SPECIAL FEATURES AND USE

January 4, 1766 JOHN BARTRAM rowed into the springhead, possibly viewing *Manatee*. January of 1989 I was lucky to see six gentle seacows *warming themselves in the run!!* JANUARY and FEBRUARY are best to glimpse these creatures. Blue Spring is a STATE PARK with camping, swimming, boating, fishing and hiking. Be sure to tour "historic" 1872 THURSBY HOUSE on grounds. Leisurely HOUSEBOATING is the *ideal way* to enjoy this "unique area." For rentals: THREE BUOYS HOUSEBOATS 1-800-262-3454.

LOCATION   Volusia County   Open to Public
Orange City, FL Off Hwy. 17   *(904) 775-3663*

BLUE HOLE SPRING

BLUE SPRING

2ND MAGNITUDE   *FLOW 60 MILLION GALLONS DAILY*

DESCRIPTION 73°

Two extensive basins nestle *deep* in a HIGH BLUFF beside Suwannee River. One vent is 50 feet deep. Water has a swirling motion and is *dark blue*. Unusual stone formations are everywhere and bottom is sandy.

SPECIAL FEATURES AND USE

If I had to CHOOSE one spring as the most stunning naturally lovely spring in Florida...this would be the ONE...!! Limestone rocks, a wide NATURAL STONE BRIDGE and deep ravine lend uncomparable beauty to the scene. This is a LAFAYETTE (pronounced Lafit) COUNTY PARK with *overnight camping* and boat ramp. On grounds are cave systems of YANA and SNAKE SINKS with air pockets, dome rooms and 20,000 ft. cave systems. Campspots perch right along the musical Suwannee. Open year round!

LOCATION   Lafayette County   Open to Public
Mayo, FL 5 miles west on Rd. 27 then north on Rd. 251 B for 2.2 miles.

BLUE HOLE SPRING

2ND MAGNITUDE   *FLOW 36.7 MILLION GALLONS DAILY*

DESCRIPTION 72°

OVAL spring. Bottom slopes from 4 ft. down to 26 ft., width is 100 ft. *A smaller pond* lies at the base of the main pool. Here are dressing rooms, *swim platform and sandy shore.* Picnic tables, concession stand nearby. Site is "within" 1783 acres of FLORIDA CAVERNS STATE PARK.

SPECIAL FEATURES AND USE

Take time to tour the *honeycomb of caves* which are as awesome as Carlsbad or Mammoth Caves. Soda straws, draperies, columns, gigantic stalactites...it's all here... INDIANS once hid in 1818 in these caves from General Jackson's army. I've visited this park about eight times. You won't tire of its unusual features. TOURS leave on the half hour.

LOCATION   Jackson County   Open to Public
Marianna, FL SR 167   *(904) 482-3632*

12

BOZELL SPRING

2ND MAGNITUDE   *FLOW 47 MILLION GALLONS DAILY*

DESCRIPTION 70°

Bozell is actually four separate springs on an 800 ft. run flowing to the CHIPOLA RIVER. Springs are numbered 1,2,3 and 4. Clear blue water has bluish tint with CATFISH and ALLIGATOR often seen. A silt cave is at 25 ft. depth.

SPECIAL FEATURES AND USE

DUCKWEED, a weensy green floating plant sometimes visible. Locals fish and swim here. Surrounding land is private property so no tie ups. Spring-fed Chipola River is well known for underwater artifact hunting. Prehistoric shark teeth and arrowheads are common. It also affords canoe buffs varied trips floating by springs such as: SAND BAG, MILL POND, DOUBLE SPRING, HAYS SPRINGS and many more that are not named!!!

LOCATION   Jackson County   Boat Access
Marianna, FL. Put-in ramp is at FLORIDA CAVERNS STATE PARK. From here go 1 mile north (upstream). Springs are on east side.   *(904) 482-3632.*

BRANFORD SPRINGS

2ND MAGNITUDE   *FLOW 19 MILLION GALLONS DAILY*

DESCRIPTION 73°

TWO POOLS (one 85 ft. wide, the other 65 ft. wide). Both are 9 ft. deep. A wooden deck and ladder give access. Spring sometimes clear, sometimes not!

SPECIAL FEATURES AND USE

Site is a local *recreation spot* for swimming, snorkeling and scuba. A DIVE SHOP and concessions are on grounds. I found the "local folks," OLD SOUTH FAMILIES, most friendly!

LOCATION   Suwanee County   Open to Public
Branford, FL Juncture of Hwy. 27 and Hwy. 129   *(904) 776-2748*

CHARLES SPRING

2ND MAGNITUDE   *FLOW 12 MILLION GALLONS DAILY*

DESCRIPTION 69°

Charles Spring is *unusual* because of the STONE BRIDGE which spans the "springhead"!! *Banks are steep* with both sections having individual boils.

SPECIAL FEATURES AND USE

Clear water with shallow sand bottom. Used for swimming or picnics.

LOCATION   Suwanee County   Open to Public
4 miles northwest of Luraville, FL Off Hwy. 252

CHASSAHOWITZKA SPRINGS

1ST MAGNITUDE   *FLOW 90 MILLION GALLONS DAILY*

DESCRIPTION 75°

Several springs discharge to the main pool. Vent is 35 ft. deep with a circular pool 150 ft. It is TIDAL flowing into 6 MILE LONG Chassahowitzka River.

SPECIAL FEATURES AND USE

Boating, fishing, swimming or SNORKELING are popular. Spring gives access to CHASSAHOWITZKA NATIONAL WILDLIFE REFUGE (1 of 12 estuarine systems) in America. I noted "playful otter" and other woods critters. CANOE TRIPS are in such demand that reservations are needed!! MAPS are available at REFUGE HEADQUARTERS on Hwy. 19.

LOCATION   Citrus County   Open to Public
Chassahowitzka, FL 7 miles south of Homosassa on U.S. 19. Canoe Rents (904) 382-2200. SPRINGS are off Hwy. 480.

CONVICT SPRING

3RD MAGNITUDE **FLOW 3.2 MILLION GALLONS DAILY**

DESCRIPTION 72°

A series of 3 CIRCULAR TERRACES descend to the boil. The 50 ft. pear-shaped pool is 20 ft. deep. Wooded site sits beside picturesque SUWANNEE RIVER. An 80 ft. CAVE SYSTEM is 30 ft. below surface. A complete DIVE COMPLEX is on grounds, and is part of JIM HOLLIS RIVER RENDEZVOUS resort!! Site was once a prison for road working "convict gangs"!

SPECIAL FEATURES AND USE

In just three years ambitious owners have turned a *wooded riverside acreage* into a FIRST CLASS WATER RESORT. Guests cavort in the SUWANNEE RIVER, rent cruise boats, swim or dive scores of nearby springs, chow down (3 squares a day) in the restaurant, relax in jacuzzis or HUGGY BEAR LOUNGE *serving 175 beer brands* or 23 wine coolers!! Canoes and game room keep the "energetic" happy. Overnight lodge or riverside accommodations offer all amenities. Reservations are best and there is an 800 telephone number good all over the U.S. of A!!!

LOCATION Lafayette County Open to Public
12.7 miles west of Branford, FL Off Rd. 27 on Rd. 354
1-800-533-5276 or (904) 294-2510

CRYSTAL SPRINGS

2ND MAGNITUDE **FLOW 39 MILLION GALLONS DAILY**

DESCRIPTION 74°

Many vents give inflow to these truly *"crystal waters."* Pool is 400 ft. long with stone outcrop and footbridge outlook. It runs into the HILLSBOROUGH RIVER.

SPECIAL FEATURES AND USE

Sentry oaks nestle over picnic tables. Abundant *aquatic plants and fish variety* provide excellent UNDERWATER PHOTO opportunities! I launched my *mini-canoe* (10 ft.) and experienced the "green cathedral" atmosphere on a 5-mile river trip!! This family-owned 400-acre PRESERVE offers bathing, canoeing, fishing and nature trails. Crystal Springs is ...out of the way... BUT ...keep it in mind!

(Continued on next page)

LOCATION   Pasco County   Open to Public
Crystal Springs, FL 3 miles south of Zephyrhills
Off Hwy. 39 on Crystal Springs Rd.   *(813) 782-5218*

CRYSTAL RIVER SPRINGS

1ST MAGNITUDE   FLOW 592.1 MILLION GALLONS DAILY

DESCRIPTION 72°
30 Springs comprise this group. Water is *mirror clear* with shafts
entering CAVES up to 60 ft. deep. Idiot's Delight, Grand Canyon,
Shark Sink and Gator Hole Springs are most popular.

SPECIAL FEATURES AND USE
Home of docile "sea cows" (MANATEE). *Superior* underwater
PHOTOGRAPHY. Crystal River is a premier DIVE SPOT in the
U.S.A. 72 degree springs afford delightful swimming.

LOCATION   Citrus County   Open to Public
Crystal River, FL Kings Bay Off U.S. 19

CRYSTAL SPRINGS

CYPRESS SPRINGS

2ND MAGNITUDE   *FLOW 52 MILLION GALLONS DAILY*

DESCRIPTION 72°

Nearly *circular* pool of 150 ft. flows into HOLMES CREEK. Deep area is 18 ft. with *majestic* CYPRESS overhanging the green boil.

SPECIAL FEATURES AND USE

Super visibility combine with *gleaming white sand bar beaches* to make this an outstanding recreation area. FLOAT TUBE trips, canoe daytrips, observing abundant *wildlife* keep outdoor buffs busy. You can't see all the native beauty in one day so stay overnight in the R.V. campgrounds, while enjoying other local "boils"... They include Hightower, Blue, Hidden, Bectom and Spring Run Springs... That should keep ya busy!

LOCATION   Washington County   Open to Public
Vernon, FL 2 miles north on Hwy. 79   *(904) 535-2960*

CYPRESS SPRINGS

DE LEON SPRINGS

2ND MAGNITUDE   *FLOW 20 MILLION GALLONS DAILY*

DESCRIPTION 73°

This is Ponce De Leon's *famed* FOUNTAIN OF YOUTH!! The 170 ft. pool is 41 ft. deep. A Spanish SUGAR MILL complete with 34 ft. *"water wheel"* was built in 1570....and *still stands.* Rolly, wooded sand hills and INDIAN BURIAL MOUNDS are nearby.

SPECIAL FEATURES AND USE

Ponce De Leon is now a STATE RECREATION AREA and well known swim spot....Ole Spanish Grist Mill is a combined mill, bakery and FLAPJACK RESTAURANT. Diners become CHEFS as they *cook pancakes at private tables with "built in griddles"!* This is one of my favorite Florida Springs...YUM YUM... Can you guess WHY?

LOCATION   Volusia County   Open to Public
DeLeon Springs, FL 5 miles north of Deland off Hwy. 17
RESTAURANT open (Daily) 9:00 am to 5:00 pm   *(904) 985-5644*

DE LEON SPRINGS (GRIST MILLWHEEL)

ELLAVILLE SPRING

2ND MAGNITUDE   *FLOW 53 MILLION GALLONS DAILY*

DESCRIPTION 70°

TURBULENT water churns out of a 30 ft. deep *cave* from high limestone BLUFFS. Water is clear. Rocks are covered with growth.

SPECIAL FEATURES AND USE

Source is from a 50 ft. fissure near to a *railroad trestle*. HUGE BOULDERS lay across the entrance and many more *span the run*. One gigantic boulder at the cave mouth causes the water to crash against it and tumble into the "run"!! Spring does not appear to be utilized. GREAT PHOTOS tho!!.

LOCATION   Suwannee County   Boat Access
Ellaville, FL east of U.S. 90 on south side of Suwannee River.

FALMOUTH SPRING

1ST MAGNITUDE   *FLOW 102.7 MILLION GALLONS DAILY*

DESCRIPTION 71°

An unusual union of SPRING and SINK occurs here. A 500 ft. run joins the two systems. All round are steep banks and heavy woods.

SPECIAL FEATURES AND USE

One CAVE reaches a depth of over 100 ft. The spring flows underground through a *cave system* to the SUWANNEE RIVER about 4 miles distant. Falmouth was hard to "track down" but I got some fine PHOTO SHOTS!

LOCATION   Suwannee County   Not Used
9 miles west of Live Oak, FL off Hwy 90

FANNIN SPRINGS

1ST MAGNITUDE   *FLOW 90 MILLION GALLONS DAILY*

DESCRIPTION 73°

There are two springs BIG FANNIN and LITTLE FANNIN. BIG FANNIN is 15 ft. deep having a 200 ft. wide pool and LITTLE FANNIN is smaller surrounded by *steep slopes* and lovely CYPRESS. Recreation area 140 acres.

SPECIAL FEATURES AND USE

Bottom is sandy and two "boils" are just 500 ft. apart. Both discharge into SUWANNEE RIVER. Sparkeling DEEP BLUE *color is striking!* Note the 600-year-old CYPRESS TREE in spring run...observation deck gives spectacular VIEWING.

LOCATION   Levy County   Open to Public April-September Fanning Springs, FL southeast side of Hwy. 19-98 river bridge.

FERN HAMMOCK SPRINGS

2ND MAGNITUDE   *FLOW 8.2 MILLION GALLONS DAILY*

DESCRIPTION 74°

Old timers called it THE AQUARIUM. A "tropical" setting stretches about the 175 by 125 ft. pool. THREE MAIN SAND BOILS give most discharge. As many as 35 more tiny sand boils add their share. Run continues to JUNIPER CREEK (a 10 mile) course to Huge Lake George.

SPECIAL FEATURES AND USE

Scenic trails are part of Juniper Springs Recreation Area. *Footbridges* span "The Aquarium." For sheer relaxing try the canoe trip down Juniper run!!

LOCATION   Marion County   Open to Public
28 miles east of Ocala, FL Hwy. 40   *(904) 625-3147*

FANNIN SPRINGS

FLETCHER SPRING

2ND MAGNITUDE   FLOW 25.8 MILLION GALLONS DAILY

DESCRIPTION 72°

Many DRY SINKS pot hole the area. Steep slopes about the 50-ft. oblong *green tinged* pool. A 450-ft. run DISAPPEARS into a SINK. Storms and river level greatly affect the water discharge.

SPECIAL FEATURES AND USE

Local folk use the site for swimming and snorkeling.

LOCATION   Lafayette County   Private Owner
10 miles southwest of Branford, FL east of Rd. 349.

GAINER SPRINGS

1ST MAGNITUDE   FLOW 112 MILLION GALLONS DAILY

DESCRIPTION 71°

Consists of 3 MAJOR SPRINGS discharging into ECONFINA CREEK where *land elevations* are 80 to 90 ft. in dense woods. Largest of three boils has *stone rocks* on the bottom.

SPECIAL FEATURES AND USE

One boil boasts a *500-foot circular pool* with a "rocky bluff" side and an ISLAND in the center. Gainer eventually flows into DEER-POINT LAKE and has been used as a Panama City water source.

LOCATION   Bay County   Not Used   Boat Access
Bennett, FL north of Hwy. 388 on Econfina River

GINNIE SPRINGS

2ND MAGNITUDE   FLOW 29 MILLION GALLONS DAILY

DESCRIPTION 72°

SIX SPRINGS well up from depths up to 70 ft. An extensive CAVE SYSTEM lies beneath *limestone ledges*. Here is famous DIVE RESORT of 200 acres (well known even outside the U.S.A.)

SPECIAL FEATURES AND USE

Eel grass, sculptured cave walls and blue-green water create magic for UNDERWATER PHOTOGRAPHY. I don't dive but there was *plenty of activity* for me! Canoeing, tubing, nature trails, boating, swimming and watching the "goings on"!!

LOCATION   Gilchrist County   Open to Public
8 mi. west of High Springs, FL Rd. 340   *(904) 454-2202*

GREEN COVE SPRINGS

3RD MAGNITUDE   *FLOW 1.9 MILLION GALLONS DAILY*

DESCRIPTION 77°

PIRATES used the spring to *fill water casks.* A small walled well has a 28-ft. visibility and streams up from a cavern 31 ft. below. Greenish water has a slight sulfur odor.

SPECIAL FEATURES AND USE

The boil now gushes 3000 gallons per minute to the CITY RUN SWIMMING POOL. *A riverside park* slopes east to the ST. JOHN'S RIVER (lots to watch here). I thought the town "quaint." Try St. John's Ave. for *post card purrty* OLD SOUTH HOMES!!

LOCATION   Clay County   Open to Public
Green Cove Springs, FL Hwy. 17 on St. John's River

GINNIE SPRINGS

GUARANTO SPRING

2ND MAGNITUDE   FLOW 8 MILLION GALLONS DAILY

DESCRIPTION 71°

An earth dam banks up the 280 by 75 ft. pool. Moss draped trees *shade the sandy banks* of the 14 ft. deep boil.

SPECIAL FEATURES AND USE

Used as a swimming hole by local residents. A dive PLATFORM floats to one side, with high grassy banks 20 ft. above the river sporting picnic tables. It is a COUNTY PARK. The morning I visited an early August mist hovered above a silent spring and slow moving Suwannee River. Note the gorgeous green CYPRESS SWAMP 1/2 mi. west of Guaranto....a photog's delight!

LOCATION   Dixie County   Open to Public
9 mi. northwest of Fanning Springs, FL off Rd. 349

GUARANTO SPRING

HAMPTON SPRINGS

4TH MAGNITUDE   *FLOW 129,600 GALLONS DAILY*

DESCRIPTION 72°

Spring is cased in a *small concrete well*. It was difficult to locate (dirt roads etc.). It flows languidly into the FENHOLLOWAY RIVER which gets its name from a Creek Indian word meaning "high bridge." The site is covered with *foundation ruins* of the once-famous HAMPTON SPRINGS HOTEL RESORT built in 1910. An historical experience overcame me as I roamed silent foundation paths where the old hotel once stood!!

SPECIAL FEATURES AND USE

The hotel had 108 *guestrooms,* a ballroom, theatre, sportsmans' clubhouse and MINERAL *swimming pool.* Surrounded by gardens and sitting on 40 acres it was said to be the ARCHITECTURAL GEM of the south. In World War II it housed military personnel. A fire destroyed the structure in 1954. *Taylor County* owns the grounds with future plans for recreation development.

LOCATION   Taylor County   Open to Public
5 mi. southwest of Perry, FL Off Hwy. 356

HART SPRINGS

2ND MAGNITUDE   *FLOW 51 MILLION GALLONS DAILY*

DESCRIPTION 73°

Two main boils discharge from a *limestone cavity.* A 27 ft. deep "swim section" has retaining walls and *dive platform.* Bottom is sandy with a 26 acre surrounding *county park.* TERRACES and FOOT-BRIDGES lead to a grassy peninsula..... VERY SCENIC.

SPECIAL FEATURES AND USE

It is possible to inch your buggy almost to the *lip of the boil.* Electrical hook-ups afford luxury camping and camper-boaters "anchor their craft" almost behind their rigs. An extra 100 acres is devoted to NATURE PATHS and boat launch right on the famed SUWANNEE RIVER!!

LOCATION   Gilchrist County   Open to Public
10 mi. north of Fanning Springs, FL Off Rd. 341

HART SPRINGS

HOLTON SPRING

1ST MAGNITUDE FLOW 311.5 MILLION GALLONS DAILY

DESCRIPTION 69°

Its *remote location* invites few visitors. The chilly pool twists for about 1 mile through upland woods to empty into SUWANNEE RIVER. It is *so canopied by majestic oaks* as not to be seen even by AIR.

SPECIAL FEATURES AND USE

An extreme fluctuation in flow is common to Holton Spring. No apparent USE is made of this spring. I challenge ANYONE to find this spring (by land) in less than 2 hours....it is only 5 miles from the paved road...I went round in circles, squares and loop-dee-loops. There are miles of enchanting Suwannee River WILDERNESS on these backroads!

LOCATION   Hamilton County   Boat Access
8 mi. northwest of Live Oak, FL Off Rd. 249 about 2.5 mi. northwest of junction of Alapaha and Suwannee Rivers.

HOMOSASSA SPRINGS

1ST MAGNITUDE   FLOW 113.8 MILLION GALLONS DAILY

DESCRIPTION 75°
Pool is 80 ft. wide, 43 ft. deep. Main vent is SALTY while South Fork vent is *freshwater.*

SPECIAL FEATURES AND USE
MAIN TOURIST ATTRACTION. A 168-ton OBSERVATORY takes visitors *into "spring boil"* to see ROSIE, a huggable manatee and an outrageous "floorshow." of fish. A zoo, trails and gardens complete the picture.

LOCATION   Citrus County   Open to Public
Homosassa Springs, FL Off U.S. 19   *(904) 628-2311*

HORNSBY SPRING

1ST MAGNITUDE   FLOW 161.6 MILLION GALLONS DAILY

DESCRIPTION 73°
Picturesque with CYPRESS TREES hovering over the grounds. A concrete swimming pool wall and a diving platform are part of the 185 ft. bathing area. Depth is 16 ft.

SPECIAL FEATURES AND USE
Spring is within a private campground, CAMP KULUQUA run by Seventh Day Adventist Church. In rain season Hornsby will flood from the SANTE FE RIVER which is a *gorgeous clear canoeing stream.* Camp Kuluqua also maintains A ZOO!

LOCATION   Alachua County Camp Kuluqua
High Springs, FL Hwy. 27   *(904) 454-1351*

HORNSBY SPRING   FL Dept. Tourism

ICHETUCKNEE SPRINGS   FL Dept. Tourism

HUNTER SPRING

2ND MAGNITUDE   *FLOW 41 MILLION GALLONS DAILY*

DESCRIPTION 77°

A grass walk leads to the crystal boil. FLow is *strong* with a wide run emptying into CRYSTAL RIVER.

SPECIAL FEATURES AND USE

A 4-acre CITY PARK nudges up to the spring. *Activity* keynotes the park... even in WINTER people are plopping in and out of the warmish water (77°). Lots of SHADE around. Showers, restrooms... even a *dock* if you don't care to come by land. Many boats bobbing about give couch potatoes lots to "ogle"!

LOCATION   Citrus County   Open to Public
Crystal River, FL (downtown) 3 blocks off Hwy. 19-98 on N.E. 1st Ave.

ICHETUCKNEE SPRINGS

1ST MAGNITUDE   *FLOW 233 MILLION GALLONS DAILY*

DESCRIPTION 73°

9 NAMED springs make up the system flowing into SANTE FE RIVER. Pool is 105 ft. long and 14 ft. deep at the vent.

SPECIAL FEATURES AND USE

Once used as a FRANCISCAN MISSION in 1600's. It is now a STATE PARK. TUBING is the "hottest" activity (1500 a day). They float *atop inner tubes* down a 6 mi. run. This is ONE of my favorite "bubbly spots"!!

LOCATION   Columbia County   Open to Public
Ft. White, FL north of Hwy. 27   *(904) 497-2511*

JUNIPER SPRINGS

2ND MAGNITUDE   *FLOW 6.5 MILLION GALLONS DAILY*

DESCRIPTION 72°

An old MILLHOUSE and undershot WATER WHEEL lend history to the 135 by 80 ft. aquamarine pool. From 17 ft. below *flumes* rush up from 3 cavities. A scenic ROCK WALL embraces the *bathing section.*

SPECIAL FEATURES AND USE

Juniper is within 382,315-acre OCALA NATIONAL FOREST. The recreational area boasts 420 acres. *Interpretive trails* lead into 66 miles of the FLORIDA HIKERS TRAIL, for serious "trampers"!! The creaking paddle wheel house is a visitors' center. CANOE RENTALS provide *lazy drifting* down seven miles of JUNIPER CREEK. Camping and swimming are highlights in these Florida forest lands!

LOCATION   Marion County   Open to Public
28 mi. east of Ocala, FL Off Rd. 40   *(904) 625-3147*

KINGSLEY LAKE SPRING

3RD MAGNITUDE   *FLOW: NO DATA*

DESCRIPTION 72°

A DEEP (45 ft.) spring with very clear water. It has the distinction of flowing into the ONLY PERFECT CIRCLE LAKE IN THE WORLD.... exactly 2 miles across.... *in any direction.* Kingsley Lake is unusual also because it *falls to 85 ft. depth in the middle.*

SPECIAL FEATURES AND USE

Kingsley Beach and Strickland Landing has entertained JACKSONVILLE folks since 1890's. HOLIDAYS may find a throng of 2000 sun seekers splashing and *whooshing down* four HIGH SLIDES into the refreshing lake!! There is camping, paddleboats and tube rentals. Sometimes carload rates apply...so pack 'em in... and come on out!! Open April to October.

LOCATION   Clay County   Open to Public
Kingsley, FL Hwy. 16 20 mi. southwest of Jacksonville
     (904) 533-2321

JUNIPER SPRINGS   FL Dept. Tourism

KINGSLEY LAKE SPRING

KINI AND RIVER SINK

1ST MAGNITUDE 　　*FLOW 114 MILLION GALLONS DAILY*

DESCRIPTION 72°

Kini erupts and flows into TWO SINKS at one end of its *large pool* (125 ft. wide 135 ft. long). A strong "WHIRLPOOL" motion is generated with one sink rotating (clockwise) and the other sink in a (counter-clockwise) movement. Depth is 24 ft.

SPECIAL FEATURES AND USE

There is much aquatic growth which is *common for sinks*. Kini Spring is UNDEVELOPED. It is on private property.

LOCATION 　　Wakulla County
12 mi. southwest of Tallahassee, FL off Rd. 369

LIME SPRING

3RD MAGNITUDE 　　　　*FLOW: NO DATA*

DESCRIPTION 72°

The center plume is barely visible. Water is coffee color and often inundated by SUWANNEE RIVER floods. Lime is 67 ft. deep, ending in an extensive CAVE.

SPECIAL FEATURES AND USE

BEAVERS sometimes use the run. The area is now part of SUWANNEE RIVER STATE PARK. Mostly used as *scenic walk* and photo opportunities. NO SWIMMING. *Three* mighty rivers meet within this park...The WITHLACOOCHEE (200 mi.)... the ALAPAHA (100 mi.) long... and the Suwannee. I have CANOED some of these backcountry systems and was awed with their unparalleled wilderness scenes!!

LOCATION 　　Suwannee County 　　Open to Public
Ellaville, FL Hwy. 90 Suwannee River Park *(904) 362-2746*
CANOE OUTPOST Live Oak, FL 　　　　*(904) 842-2192*

LITHIA SPRINGS

2ND MAGNITUDE   FLOW 33 MILLION GALLONS DAILY

DESCRIPTION 76°

TWIN POOLS of Lithia Major and Lithia Minor well up from a 16-ft.-deep orifice. A raised bank leads to a *peninsula overlooking* clear, sand-bottomed waters which flow a short distance into the ALAFIA RIVER. Stone ledges are visible.

SPECIAL FEATURES AND USE

Lithia is a recreational "GEM" and rather *unknown*. It is a county park (160 acres) ...camp spots (right on the river)... and *highlight of daily events* is a 4-HOUR TUBING TRIP with put-in at Alderman's Ford on Hwy. 39. Lithia is a marvelous GETAWAY PLACE!

LOCATION   Hillsborough County   Open to Public
20 mi. southeast of Tampa, FL off Rd. 640 on Lithia Springs Rd.
(813) 689-2139

LITHIA SPRINGS

LITTLE RIVER SPRINGS

2ND MAGNITUDE   *FLOW 54 MILLION GALLONS DAILY*

DESCRIPTION 72°

Basin is large with *bare stone* and sand bottom. HEAVY WOODS are all around. A 15 ft. deep entrance reveals an *extensive* underground CAVE SYSTEM. One passage leads 800 ft. to the "Florida Room."

SPECIAL FEATURES AND USE

Swim basin of 3 ft. or so is perfect for "little people" and summer romps! Submerged caves provide some of Florida's FINEST DIVING. Exploring extends over 1200 ft. and descends over 100 ft. for experienced diver. It is a County Park used for picnics, bathing and snorkeling. Info call *(904) 776-2748*

LOCATION   Suwannee County   Open to Public
4 mi. north of Branford, FL west of Rd. 129.

LITTLE SALT SPRING

4TH MAGNITUDE   *FLOW 594,688 GALLONS DAILY*

DESCRIPTION 77°

Historically significant because of *human skeletons* uncovered on a 90 ft. deep ledge. BONES WERE DATED OVER 5,000 years old. A 250 ft. pool is ringed by thick cabbage palms and scrub oak. A 1½ mi. "run" ends in a slough and then to MYAKKA RIVER.

SPECIAL FEATURES AND USE

I spent one memorable NEW YEARS EVE "hunting up" this spring. Ripped my jeans *climbing the fence,* my buggy got *stuck in the sugar sand* and a pair of my glasses lie deep in that mysterious pool......yet, I am happy I was able to view this natural gem in its pristine state!! Today state archeologists study Little Salt's 250 ft. depths and *cave system.* Sarasota County, State of Florida and Universities maintain a study center on site.

LOCATION   Sarasota County
North Port, FL east of Hwy. 41 (2) mi. northeast of Warm Mineral Springs — East on Biscayne, South on Price (near school grounds).

LITTLE RIVER SPRINGS

MANATEE SPRINGS

1ST MAGNITUDE   FLOW 116.9 MILLION GALLONS DAILY

DESCRIPTION 73°

Springhead is 100 feet across, 45 ft. deep. Boil is surrounded by *cypress*. A 1,200 ft. spring run discharges into the SUWANNEE RIVER which flows 23 miles into the Gulf of Mexico.

SPECIAL FEATURES AND USE

It is a State Park of 2075 acres with a unique SINK TRAIL TOUR. There is camping, fishing, boating. CANOE RENTALS available. Diving allowed. I especially enjoyed the swamp boardwalk and observation deck overlooking the SUWANNEE!!

LOCATION   Levy County   Open to Public
Chiefland, FL off U.S. 19 on Rd. 320   *(904) 493-4288*

McBRIDE SLOUGH SPRINGS

4TH MAGNITUDE   *FLOW UNDETERMINED*

DESCRIPTION 72°

Several shallow springs gurgle up in a *wooded marshy area* beside busy Hwy. 267. Source water is from WAKULLA SPRINGS nearby. When sunlight pierces the heavy canopy the small pools and run take on a blue-green tint.

SPECIAL FEATURES AND USE

A short path on the north side of Rd. 267 leads to the boils. *Blooming aquatic growth* is abundant. There are no facilities but this does not stop locals (in large numbers) from enjoying *summer afternoon dips* in the SLOUGH!!

LOCATION   Wakulla County   Open to Public
Wakulla, FL 1½ mi. west on Rd. 267 at McBRIDE SLOUGH BRIDGE.

MORRISON SPRING

2ND MAGNITUDE   *FLOW 40 MILLION GALLONS DAILY*

DESCRIPTION 76°

Located in DENSE WOODS. Spring wells up from three CAVES (one is 300 ft. deep, another is 100 ft. down and the third is 50 ft. below). *These caves* end in a HUGE ROOM of unspecified dimension. Flow is into CHOCTAWHATCHEE RIVER.

SPECIAL FEATURES AND USE

Large basin is popular for swimming, fishing and diving. A *dive concession and camping* are on grounds.

LOCATION   Walton County   Open to Public
5 mi. northeast of Redbay, FL off Hwy. 81   *(904) 836-4223*

McBRIDE SLOUGH SPRINGS

MORRISON SPRING

NAKED SPRING

2ND MAGNITUDE   FLOW 18.2 MILLION GALLONS DAILY

DESCRIPTION 73°

It is 75 ft. in diameter and 12 ft. deep. Gentle flumes issue from three crevices. *Water is clean.*

SPECIAL FEATURES AND USE

....HERE'S THE STORY.... Back in "olden times" the well-to-do folks who could sport *bathing apparel* swam in Blue Springs....those who couldn't afford trunks followed the woods path to SKINNY DIP at NAKED SPRING!

LOCATION   Gilchrist County   Open to Public
9 mi. west of High Springs, FL Off Rd. 340
450 ft. east of BLUE SPRINGS

NATURAL BRIDGE SPRING

1ST MAGNITUDE   FLOW 68.5 MILLION GALLONS DAILY

DESCRIPTION 68°

Vent is 40 ft. deep and 40 ft. across bounded by *heavy* SWAMP and forest. Stream bed has heavy growth of "eelgrass" and disappears into a SINKHOLE 700 ft. downstream. Sink is 37 ft. deep.

SPECIAL FEATURES AND USE

Natural Bridge is a STATE HISTORIC SITE. A *monument* commemorates a "civil war battle." On March 6, 1865, cadets from West Florida Seminary (FLORIDA STATE UNIVERSITY) teamed with other Confederate defenders to stop Union Forces from capturing Tallahassee. In the fight 11 men died and 135 were wounded. SCUBA DIVING, SNORKELING and FISHING are allowed.

LOCATION   Leon County   Open to Public
8 mi. southeast of Tallahassee, FL on Natural Bridge Rd. (SR 354).

NEWPORT SPRINGS

3RD MAGNITUDE   *FLOW 5.3 MILLION GALLONS DAILY*

DESCRIPTION 73°

A wooden dam barricades one end of the 100 by 50 ft. pool. Opening is a *limestone ledge* at depth of 8 ft.

SPECIAL FEATURES AND USE

Subject to TIDES and has a sulfur odor. Local residents use the spring to swim. NEWPORT hides a lot of HISTORY....if you scout around, you'll dig some up!!

LOCATION   Wakulla County   Open to Public
Newport, FL 15 mi. southeast of Tallahassee. North of Hwy. 98 take road north .1 mile on west side of St. Mark's River bridge.

NEWPORT SPRINGS

OTTER SPRINGS

2ND MAGNITUDE   *FLOW 10 MILLION GALLONS DAILY*

DESCRIPTION 73°

Two fissures (31 and 23 ft. deep) rise to a *clear pool* (135 ft.) wide and ten ft. deep. Stream bed meanders into SUWANNEE RIVER.

SPECIAL FEATURES AND USE

Otter Springs is a private RESORT and is home to about four "outstanding" BLUEGRASS FESTIVALS each year. Canoe rentals, camping, hike trails, an AIRSTRIP, *canteen* and *"spring splashing"* keep visitors happy!

LOCATION   Gilchrist County   Open to Public
Trenton, FL Hwy. 349   *(904) 463-2696*

PEACOCK SPRINGS

2ND MAGNITUDE   *FLOW 9.6 MILLION GALLONS DAILY*

DESCRIPTION 73°

Three vents are surrounded by dense *cypress woods and swamp*. Pool is 300 ft. long and 75 ft. wide. Lovely DARK BLUE water is *clear*. A cave system ranges from 40 ft. to 20 ft. deep.

SPECIAL FEATURES AND USE

In 1989 these 200 ACRES became PEACOCK SPRINGS STATE PARK. Colors "fan out" from the waters just like a strutting peacock. A 1½-mile LILY PAD run makes scenic snorkeling. Do make TIME for exploring the other NUMEROUS SPRINGS within the park....they are ORANGE, OLSEN, BONNET, POT HOLE, WATER HOLE, CHALLENGE and of course PEACOCK SPRINGS.

LOCATION   Suwannee County   Open to Public
Luraville, FL Hwy. 51   *(904) 776-2310*

OTTER SPRINGS

POE SPRINGS

2ND MAGNITUDE   *FLOW 60 MILLION GALLONS DAILY*

DESCRIPTION 73°

A *mix of four boils* issues from a depth of 17 ft. to form a "round" pool 90 ft. across. Background is the SANTA FE RIVER.

SPECIAL FEATURES AND USE

Poe is part of 100-acre SANTA FE RIVER PARK. A *cypress nature walk* meanders to a large blue-green swim spot. It is always chock full of sun seekers who are perfecting their cannonballing and rope swinging styles!! I would put Poe Springs in the *top 10* of my "FAVORITE BUBBLIES"!

LOCATION   Alachua County   Open to Public
High Springs, FL off Rd. 236 West on Rd. 340 for 3 miles.

POE SPRINGS

PONCE DE LEON SPRINGS

2ND MAGNITUDE   FLOW 12 MILLION GALLONS DAILY

DESCRIPTION 68°

A KIDNEY FORM pool measures 100 by 75 ft. THREE VENTS lead to *underground caverns* 19 ft. below. A short "run" rushes into SANDY CREEK. Unusual is the "underwater" NATURAL BRIDGE formed by 2 cave openings!!

SPECIAL FEATURES AND USE

The "picturesque" site is a STATE RECREATION PARK offering bathing, showers, dressing rooms and picnic fun facilities! NO SCUBA ALLOWED. I found the tiny hamlet of PONCE DE LEON quite charming... I shall surely return!!

LOCATION   Holmes County   Open to Public
Ponce De Leon, FL Between I-10 and Hwy. 90 Off Rd. 181
(904) 836-4281

RAINBOW SPRINGS

1ST MAGNITUDE   FLOW 493.2 MILLION GALLONS DAILY

DESCRIPTION 70°

Discharge is from four deep cavities into a headpool of 250 ft. Water is unusually "soft" and courses 5.4 miles through *wooded hills* to WITHLACOOCHEE RIVER. Probably the most BEAUTEOUS spring in our state!! I found the aquamarine waters "enchanting."

SPECIAL FEATURES AND USE

74° spring has *abundant* aquatic life. RAINBOW RIVER is on Florida's "outstanding river" list and a well known DIVE spot. TUBERS love the *float* down 3 mile Blue Run. Put-ins or access for canoe, tube rental or diving is at K.P. HOLE 3 miles north of Dunnellon off Hwy 41. State Park system is dickering to buy RAINBOW — keep your fingers crossed!

LOCATION   Marion County   Public Access above
4 miles north of Dunnellon, FL off Hwy. 41

RAINBOW SPRINGS

ROCK SPRINGS

2ND MAGNITUDE   *FLOW 42 MILLION GALLONS DAILY*

DESCRIPTION 75°

Springs spurt from a partially submerged *cave* at bottom of a 17 ft. high STONE BLUFF. Rock ledges and green wooded ravines combine with a large swim area to make the spot most SCENIC. The run meanders 8 miles to WEKIVA RIVER and eventually into ST. JOHN'S RIVER.

SPECIAL FEATURES AND USE

TUBING the run is THE #1 ACTIVITY...I began as a kid in 1948... *I'm still at it!!* Rock Springs is a 200-acre county park (KELLY PARK). It borders an 8750-acre STATE PRESERVE. There is canoeing, camping and nature trails.

LOCATION   Orange County   Open to Public
Apopka, FL off SR 435. Kelly Park *(407) 889-4179*
ROCK SPRINGS PRESERVE *(904) 383-3311.*

ROYAL SPRING

3RD MAGNITUDE   *FLOW: NO DATA*

DESCRIPTION 72°

A 200 by 100 ft. pool. Vegetation often covers it. STEEP SLOPES hem pool edges and are thick with pine and oak trees.

SPECIAL FEATURES AND USE

A retaining wall and dock are evident. A cave is 50 ft. down the side of a *stone cliff.* FLOW IS VERY LOW!! To left of the run is a boat launch. The area is now a COUNTY PARK.

LOCATION   Suwannee County   Open to Public
12 miles northwest of Branford, FL Off SR 349   *(904) 935-1141*

RUM ISLAND SPRING

UNKNOWN MAGNITUDE   *FLOW UNDETERMINED*

DESCRIPTION 72°

It is small, filling a basin of about 50 ft. across with *looking glass clear water*. 12 ft. is maximum depth.

SPECIAL FEATURES AND USE

You may imagine just HOW this spring, Rum Island, got its name... today though it is a quite respectable COLUMBIA COUNTY PARK. You will find picnic tables and a *boat ramp* which flows to the SANTA FE RIVER. Late AUGUST was when I visited and *colorful aquatic plants* floated mid stream with a green backdrop of tall *lacy cypress giants*.

LOCATION   Columbia County   Open to Public
High Springs, FL 2 mi. west on Rd. 27 west of Santa Fe River bridge, go to Rum Island Spring Rd. (paved), 2.1 mi. to dirt road at grocery store. Follow dirt road 2 mi. to the spring.

RUNNING SPRINGS

2ND MAGNITUDE   *FLOW 49.7 MILLION GALLONS DAILY*

DESCRIPTION 71°

So called because of its SWIFT MOVEMENT! West Spring and East Spring have *steep limestone walls*. Numerous boils pop up in the "fast moving" stream bed.

SPECIAL FEATURES AND USE

RAPIDS are visible in the shallow swim pool!! Natural STONE BRIDGES make Running Springs a *beauty spot*. Water was irresistible...I plunged in for a cool-down on a hot afternoon...b-r-r-r!!!

LOCATION   Suwannee County   Open to Public
Luraville, FL east of Hwy. 51   *(904) 776-2310*

RUNNING SPRINGS

SAINT MARK'S SPRING

1ST MAGNITUDE   FLOW 330.4 MILLION GALLONS DAILY

DESCRIPTION 71°

An 87-ft. springpool is *unique* because it divides into TWO RUNS (one being 35 ft. deep), the other only 13 ft. deep! Water flows *"over and through"* cavernous LIMESTONE and at peak rains St. Mark's River *inundates* the boil.

SPECIAL FEATURES AND USE

Springflow greatly varies from year to year. Locals fish here. I took my *tiny houseboat* upriver and found the TOPOGRAPHY fascinating. You could walk across ROCK LEDGES spanning the river near its headwaters.

LOCATION   Leon County   Boat Access
13 mi. south of Tallahassee, FL 6 mi. east on Natural Bridge Rd. (354) or BOAT RAMP and CAMPGROUND at Newport, FL on Hwy. 98.

SALT SPRING

2ND MAGNITUDE   *FLOW 49.8 MILLION GALLONS DAILY*

DESCRIPTION 75°

ROCK FLOOR has nine fissures sending up bubbling jets. Tree-lined slopes encompass the 110-ft. swimming area which is only 4 to 6 ft. deep.

SPECIAL FEATURES AND USE

Part of STATE PARK LANDS. Grassbeds reveal water critters and curious plant life. BLUE CRABS are numerous *in (nearby) Lake George.* A marvelous green jungle RUN extends for 4 MILES to hook up with LAKE GEORGE.... it's pur-r-r-fect for SNORKEL-ING. Day use only.

LOCATION   Marion County   Open to Public in 1990
28 mi. northeast of Ocala, FL Hwy. 314

SALT SPRINGS

SILVER SPRINGS

1ST MAGNITUDE   *FLOW 532 MILLION GALLONS DAILY*

DESCRIPTION 76°

Spring pool is 250 ft. diameter and source for 5 mile SILVER RIVER which flows into *scenic tropical* OKLAWAHA RIVER. Cave mouth is 5 ft. high, 135 ft. wide, with some caverns extending 55 ft. deep.

SPECIAL FEATURES AND USE

Major Tourist Attraction. World-famous Glass Bottom Boat Ride over 17 gorgeous "boils." Gator Shows, Reptile Institute and AFRICAN WILDLIFE GARDENS.

LOCATION   Marion County   Open to Public
Ocala, FL SR 40   *1-800-342-0297*

SILVER GLEN SPRINGS

1ST MAGNITUDE   *FLOW 72.3 MILLION GALLONS DAILY*

DESCRIPTION 74°

About 3 crevices in the rocks send up a very FORCEFUL BOIL from 28 feet below. A short spring run dumps into LAKE GEORGE. Pool is 200 ft. around with surrounding *"tropical woods."*

SPECIAL FEATURES AND USE

Indians left large SNAIL SHELL MOUNDS and *Indian remains* and *artifacts* of this era have been found near the springs. Lake George is an outstanding CRABBING lake...I recall taking home five dozen with just two or three hours effort one sunny afternoon.

LOCATION   Marion County   Open to Public
9 mi. northwest of Astor, FL off Hwy. 19

SUWANNEE SPRINGS

2ND MAGNITUDE   FLOW 15.5 MILLION GALLONS DAILY

DESCRIPTION 70°

(SIX SPRINGS) huddle at the *very edge* of the SUWANNEE RIVER. They are enclosed by a 110-year-old RIVER ROCK WALL. Water is green and gin-clear. *Rock steps* descend into the bathing boil where sloping sandy banks provide much room for "sunning."

SPECIAL FEATURES AND USE

In early 1900's "snow birds" flocked to SUWANNEE SPRINGS HEALTH RESORT. Hotels lined river banks and a *trolleycar* hustled up and down the tracks between rail depot, hotels and the springs. West of the paved entrance is the OCTAGONAL ROCK HOME OF GOVERNOR DAY built in 1890 of *stone hauled up from riverbed.* On southwest side of new bridge is SPIRIT OF SUWANNEE campground (500 scenic acres). The SUWANNEE RIVER in this section just does not get any more beautiful!! TRY TO SEE SOME OF IT.

LOCATION   Suwannee County   Open to Public

Suwannee Springs, FL 5 mi. north of Live Oak Off Rd. 129 South side of NEW BRIDGE. Springs on dirt road on southeast side of OLD BRIDGE.

SUWANNEE SPRINGS   FL Dept. Tourism

TELFORD SPRING

2ND MAGNITUDE　　*FLOW 22 MILLION GALLONS DAILY*

DESCRIPTION 70°

A deep RAVINE topped by *dense tropical foliage* hugs the shallow 30 ft. wide pool. Separate "boils" issue from two rock fissures to the blue pool, then jets into crystal shallows to trickle to the Suwannee River close by.

SPECIAL FEATURES AND USE

This has been MAYO'S ole swimmin' hole for "donkies years." HIGH SAND BANKS make for *marvelous photography.* CANOE RENTALS are nearby. A picnic area is beside the river on southeast side of bridge over the Suwannee on Rd. 51.

LOCATION　　Suwannee County　　Open to Public
Luraville, FL 20 mi. southwest of Live Oak off Rd. 51, northeast side of Suwannee River by bridge.

TROY SPRINGS

1ST MAGNITUDE　　*FLOW 132.5 MILLION GALLONS DAILY*

DESCRIPTION 72°

A very DEEP spring (80 ft.) and quite large (200 ft. long, 100 ft. wide). Unusually *clear* water. LOGS can plainly be seen on the *sandy bottom.* Steep banks surround the area.

SPECIAL FEATURES AND USE

The *sunken hull* of the STEAMBOAT, MADISON can be viewed. Its bow points to the "springhead." It was a CONFEDERATE gunboat cornered on the Suwannee River. The captain *scuttled* it to avoid a capture by UNION soldiers.....I had a most difficult time "locating" this spring (by land) but the effort was worth it! Be sure to close ALL ROAD GATES. It is used for swimming, scuba or snorkeling but no public facilities.

LOCATION　　Lafayette County　　Open to Public
6 mi. northwest of Branford, FL Off Hwy 20 on sand road.

TELFORD SPRING

TROY SPRINGS (NOTE GUNBOAT HULL)

VORTEX SPRING

2ND MAGNITUDE   FLOW 4.5 MILLION GALLONS DAILY

DESCRIPTION 72°

Water is *clear* and one CAVE descends 125 ft. Vortex is 250 ft. (ACROSS) with *shallow sand areas* for bathing. *Limestone ledges* hover near the vent.

SPECIAL FEATURES AND USE

A MARINE RUN is lovely for SNORKELERS. A commercial DIVE SHOP is on grounds. *Some caves* can be explored over 700 ft.! Main pool is *50 ft. deep.* A restaurant, picnic tables and bath houses offer convenience.

LOCATION   Holmes County   Open to Public
4 mi. north of Ponce De Leon, FL off Hwy. 81   *(904) 836-4979*

WACISSA SPRINGS

1ST MAGNITUDE   FLOW 251.4 MILLION GALLONS DAILY

DESCRIPTION 70°

12 springs dot the first two miles of Wacissa River. Waters are CLEAR but aquatic growth is a problem. One mile north of the springhead land becomes HILLY *rising over 100 ft. above the lowlands!*

SPECIAL FEATURES AND USE

St. Joe Paper Company is a large land owner along the river. The river is a STATE CANOE TRAIL offering six hours of *wild back-country beauty.* The trail "twists" through AUCILLA GAME MANAGEMENT AREA emptying into Aucilla River near Hwy. 98.

LOCATION   Jefferson County   Open to Public
15 mi. south of Tallahassee, FL off Hwy. 59

WAKULLA SPRINGS

1ST MAGNITUDE   *FLOW 252 MILLION GALLONS DAILY*

DESCRIPTION 73°

One of the world's largest. Main Spring has a depth of 225 ft. while SALLY WARD spring reaches to 295 ft. GRAND CANYON CAVE extends 600 ft. Water has outstanding "clarity" with LIGHT *reaching* to 69 ft.

SPECIAL FEATURES AND USE

Located in 2900-acre WAKULLA STATE PARK. A 1937 "old world" LODGE with *marble floors* and massive fireplace overlooks the boil. SWIMMING, Glass Bottom Boat Rides or canoeing WAKULLA RIVER'S magnolia lined banks are popular with guests. I highly advocate the "gourmet experience" turned out daily by the lodge's professional chefs!!

LOCATION   Wakulla County   Open to Public
15 mi. south of Tallahassee, FL on Rd. 267   *(904) 640-7263*

WACISSA SPRINGS

WAKULLA SPRINGS   FL Dept. Tourism

WALDO SPRINGS

3RD MAGNITUDE   FLOW 2.8 MILLION GALLONS DAILY

DESCRIPTION 71°

CYPRESS *flatlands* border the 60 ft. boil. Clear water has 9 ft. depth and partial LIMESTONE FLOOR.

SPECIAL FEATURES AND USE

Bathers can view numerous SEEPS in the sandy bottom. Stream bed runs into the FENHOLLOWAY RIVER. Used by local residents for SWIMMING.

LOCATION   Taylor County   Boat Access
4 mi. southwest of Perry, FL Off Rd. 359

WARM MINERAL SPRINGS

3RD MAGNITUDE   *FLOW 5 MILLION GALLONS DAILY*

DESCRIPTION 87°

Source of the HOT *salty* water comes from 3000 ft. deep BOULDER ZONE in the state aquifer. The famous diver, BILL ROYAL, discovered (on a 43-ft. ledge) human remains *carbon dated* over 10,000 years old. This spring is SO RARE in formation and history it has been put on the NATIONAL REGISTRY OF HISTORIC PLACES.

SPECIAL FEATURES AND USE

This is a privately owned HEALTH RESORT... 250 ft. swimming pool has "high mineral" content...DEPTH exceeds 245 ft. STALACTITES and CATHEDRAL CHAMBERS are found. A phenomenon concerns water visibility..... daytime is often cloudy but overnight spring *can have clarity from almost 200 ft. below!!* Ongoing explorations are done by State of Florida and the University of Florida. BATHING and PICNICKING are allowed.

LOCATION   Sarasota County   Open to Public
North Port, FL Hwy. 41   *(813) 426-1692*

WARM MINERAL SPRINGS

WEEKI WACHEE

1ST MAGNITUDE   FLOW 113 MILLION GALLONS DAILY

DESCRIPTION 75°

Large spring pool (250 ft. long by 150 ft. wide) and 60 ft. deep. CAVE WALLS are *deeply scalloped* from turbulent water discharge.

SPECIAL FEATURES AND USE

Since 1947 a main tourist attraction. LIVE MERMAID SHOW OF 30 min. 3 TALL FLUMES provide *exciting plunges* into the "boil" for visitors. Birds of Prey Show is excellent (20 min.) and a WILDERNESS RIVER CRUISE (30 min.) glides through *jungley scenes.*

LOCATION   Hernando County   Open to Public
12 mi. southwest of Brooksville, FL off U.S. 19   *(800) 342-0297*

WEKIVA SPRINGS

2ND MAGNITUDE   FLOW 35.5 MILLION GALLONS DAILY

DESCRIPTION 72°

An *extremely beautiful* complex of three uneven pools connected by several ROCK BRIDGES. Smallest pool is 30 feet, the largest is 189 ft. with 30 ft. depth. One pool has a ROCK ISLAND *in the center!!*

SPECIAL FEATURES AND USE

Until 1988 this gorgeous spring setting was used by locals for recreation. It is now in private hands and used for commercial water supply. There is NO PUBLIC ACCESS. A fun tubing trip is nearby at HENRY BECK COUNTY PARK with take out at Rd. 326 bridge over the Wekiva Run. Park is quite scenic with *steps leading to clear sand swim banks.* Summer barbecues under cool oaks are popular at this remote park.

LOCATION   Levy County   Private Ownership
Gulf Hammock, FL off Hwy. 19, northeast on Rd. 326 for 4.9 mi. at electric power transmission line. HENRY BECK PARK is 2 mi. west of Wekiva Springs on Rd. 343.

WEKIWA SPRINGS

2ND MAGNITUDE   *FLOW 48 MILLION GALLONS DAILY*

DESCRIPTION 75°

A long, high sloping grassy hill overlooks a kidney-bean-like pool of 200 ft. length. *A footbridge* traverses the stream where TIMUCUAN INDIANS once speared fish. The "fish crowded" boil comes from five caves 15 ft. below.

SPECIAL FEATURES AND USE

Springs are focal point of WEKIWA SPRINGS STATE PARK (6400 acres). Rangers told me they *occasionally* sight BLACK BEAR in this preserve only 15 miles from bustling Orlando!!! There is camping, canoeing, swimming, *13 miles of hiking* or bring your "HOSS"... there are 9 miles of Horseback Paths.

LOCATION   Orange County   Open to Public
Altamonte Springs, FL off SR 436   *(407) 889-3140*

WHITE SPRINGS

2ND MAGNITUDE   *FLOW 25.8 MILLION GALLONS DAILY*

DESCRIPTION 70°

Once a "world famed" health spa, users claimed there were *50 minerals* in spring water. Waters issue from a limestone cavern 39 ft. deep. *Springhouse foundation* "ruins" can still be seen. Here was the BATH HOUSE used by presidents and the rich.

SPECIAL FEATURES AND USE

In 1970's I saw the COLONIAL HOTEL (built in 1900) before it was torn down.... she was a multi-storied, wide-porched beauty queen!! Springs still flow copiously but not used for SWIMMING. They are part of 250-acre STEPHEN FOSTER MEMORIAL PARK. There are river boat rides, a pink CARILLON tower with *daily concerts* and a museum with belongings of the renowned composer. I lunched under mossed oaks watching PADDLE WHEEL replicas chug up the musical Suwannee.

LOCATION   Hamilton County   Open to Public
White Springs, FL Stephen Foster Memorial   *(904) 397-2733*

WORTHINGTON SPRING

3RD MAGNITUDE   *FLOW 232,704 GALLONS DAILY*

DESCRIPTION 71°

A low woody area embraces the flood prone spring. An abandoned concrete pool (90 ft. by 50 ft.) was once a private HOTEL RECREATION RESORT. In 1989 (3) rickity dressing cabins stood sentinel on the hillside.

SPECIAL FEATURES AND USE

North edge of pool has a nine ft. limestone depth and murky blue-green appearance. Maximum cavern depth is 41 ft. NO USE IS MADE OF THE SPRING. Youngsters use the "lowland" for O.R.V. revving around!

LOCATION   Union County

Worthington Springs, FL 25 mi. northwest of Gainesville Hwy. 121 (northwest side of bridge).

SWEETWATER SPRING (JUNIPER CREEK)

TUBING TRIPS

1. CYPRESS SPRINGS........2-3 hours 3 mile float on remote Holmes Creek. Washington County at Vernon, FL (904) 535-2960

2. LITHIA SPRINGS..........A 4 hour float on 5 miles of pristine Alafia River. White sandbars ideal for picnics. Put-in at ALDERMAN'S FORD PARK on Rd. 39. Take out is Lithia Springs. Hillsborough County 25 mi. southeast of Tampa, FL (813) 689-2139

3. ICHETUCKNEE SPRINGS..Choice of 3 trips 1 hr, 1½ hr, or 2 hrs (mid point take out) with FERRY SERVICE. Scenic 6 mile "run." Columbia County. Ft. White, FL (904) 497-2511

4. RAINBOW SPRINGS.......A 2 hour drift on 4 mile "Blue Run." Put-in at K.P. HOLE 3 miles north of Dunnellon, FL. Tube rentals at K.P. Hole. Marion County, Dunnellon, FL.

5. ROCK SPRINGS...........A 1 mile float with easy walk back trail. Most popular in summer so come early. Kelly Park in Orange County Apopka, FL (407) 889-4179.

6. GINNIE SPRINGS..........A 2 mile "drift" on lazy Santa Fe River. Put-in at Devil's Spring. Explore 6 other springs enroute. High Springs, FL (904) 454-2202.

FLORIDA'S SUBMARINE SPRINGS

GEORGIA

FLORIDA

EXPLANATION

1. Bear Creek Spring
2. Cedar Island Spring
3. Cedar Island Springs
4. Choctawhatchee Springs
5. Crays Rise
6. Crescent Beach Submarine
7. Crystal Beach Spring
8. Freshwater Cave
9. Mud Hole Submarine Spring
10. Ocean Hole Spring
11. Ray Hole Spring
12. Red Snapper Sink
13. Spring Creek Springs
14. Tarpon Springs
15. The Jewfish Hole
16. Unnamed Spring No. 4

Springs Along The Suwannee River

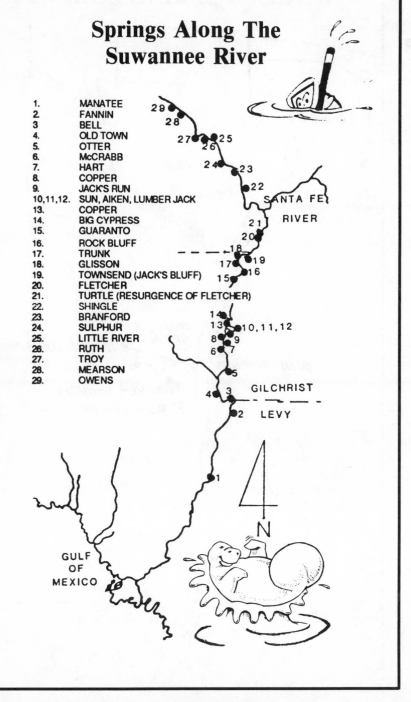

1.	MANATEE
2	FANNIN
3	BELL
4.	OLD TOWN
5.	OTTER
6.	McCRABB
7.	HART
8.	COPPER
9.	JACK'S RUN
10,11,12.	SUN, AIKEN, LUMBER JACK
13.	COPPER
14.	BIG CYPRESS
15.	GUARANTO
16.	ROCK BLUFF
17.	TRUNK
18.	GLISSON
19.	TOWNSEND (JACK'S BLUFF)
20.	FLETCHER
21.	TURTLE (RESURGENCE OF FLETCHER)
22.	SHINGLE
23.	BRANFORD
24.	SULPHUR
25.	LITTLE RIVER
26.	RUTH
27.	TROY
28.	MEARSON
29.	OWENS

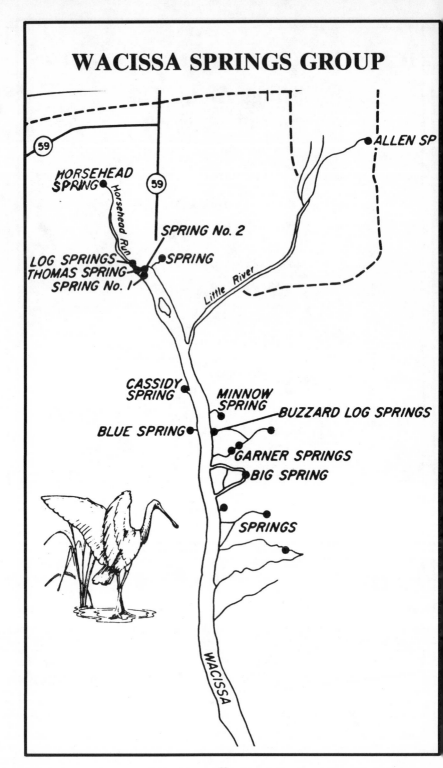

WACISSA SPRINGS GROUP

59

ALLEN SP

HORSEHEAD SPRING

59

Horsehead Run

SPRING No. 2

LOG SPRINGS
THOMAS SPRING
SPRING No. 1

SPRING

Little River

CASSIDY SPRING

MINNOW SPRING

BUZZARD LOG SPRINGS

BLUE SPRING

GARNER SPRINGS

BIG SPRING

SPRINGS

WACISSA

ICHETUCKNEE SPRINGS GROUP

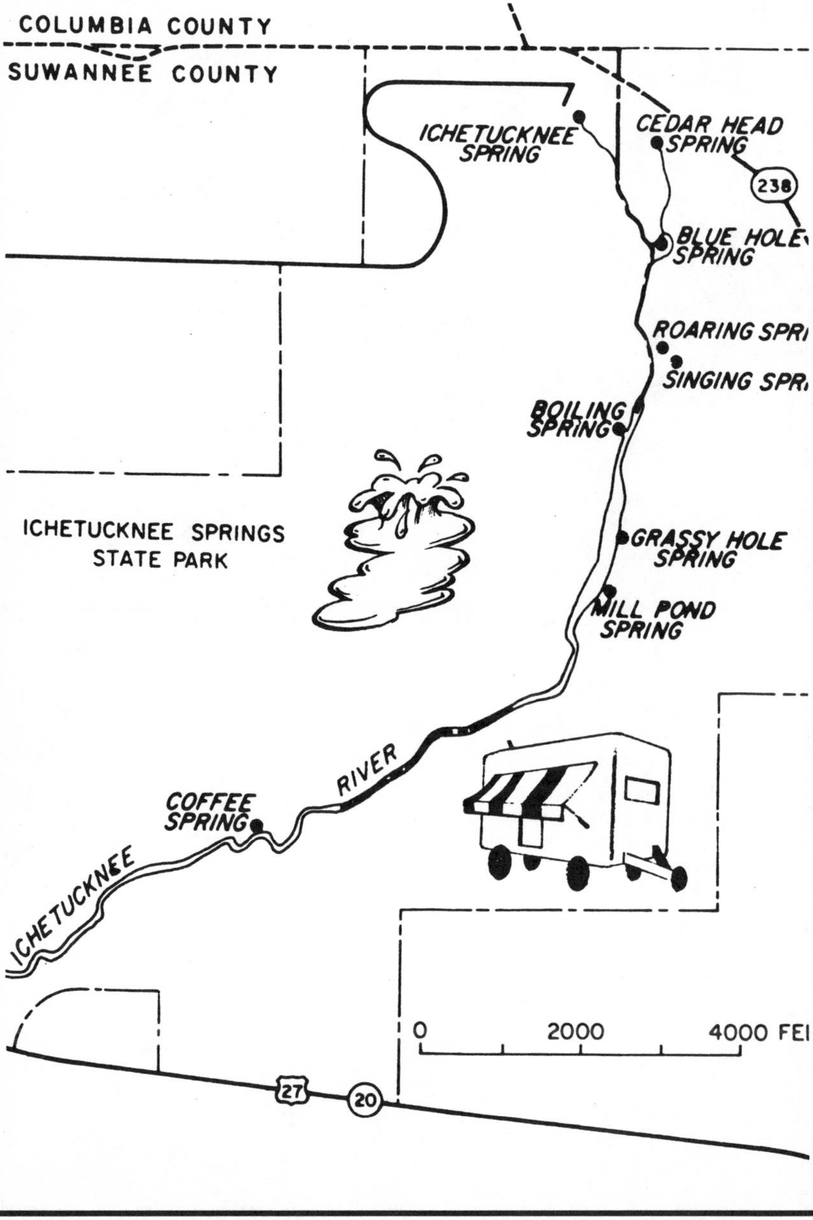

COLUMBIA COUNTY

SUWANNEE COUNTY

ICHETUCKNEE SPRING

CEDAR HEAD SPRING

238

BLUE HOLE SPRING

ROARING SPRI

SINGING SPR

BOILING SPRING

ICHETUCKNEE SPRINGS STATE PARK

GRASSY HOLE SPRING

MILL POND SPRING

RIVER

COFFEE SPRING

ICHETUCKNEE

0   2000   4000 FEI

27   20

Index Map
for the
Florida Canoe Trail System

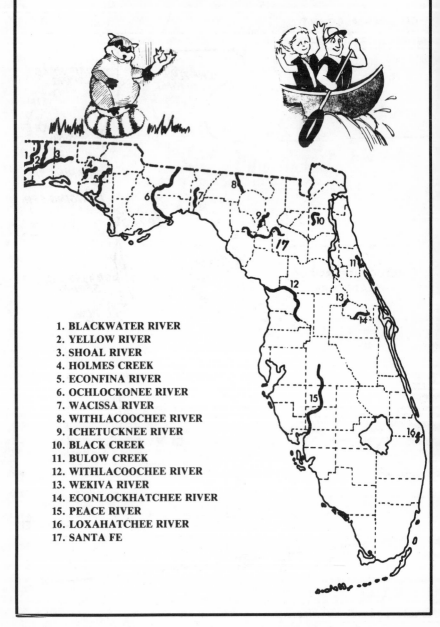

1. BLACKWATER RIVER
2. YELLOW RIVER
3. SHOAL RIVER
4. HOLMES CREEK
5. ECONFINA RIVER
6. OCHLOCKONEE RIVER
7. WACISSA RIVER
8. WITHLACOOCHEE RIVER
9. ICHETUCKNEE RIVER
10. BLACK CREEK
11. BULOW CREEK
12. WITHLACOOCHEE RIVER
13. WEKIVA RIVER
14. ECONLOCKHATCHEE RIVER
15. PEACE RIVER
16. LOXAHATCHEE RIVER
17. SANTA FE